Literary Gems

Series I. to IV. (comprising 24 books) now ready

For full list, see end of this volume

Literary Gems

L'Allegro
and
Il Penseroso

together with

The Sonnets and Odes

By

John Milton

New York and London
G. P. Putnam's Sons
The Knickerbocker Press

Electrotyped, Printed, and Bound by
The Knickerbocker Press, New York
G. P. Putnam's Sons

CONTENTS.

L'ALLEGRO

L'ALLEGRO.

By John Milton.

HENCE, loathed Melancholy,
Of Cerberus and blackest Midnight born
In Stygian cave forlorn,
'Mongst horrid shapes, and shrieks, and sights unholy!
Find out some uncouth cell,
Where brooding Darkness spreads his jealous wings,
And the night-raven sings;
There, under ebon shades and low-browed rocks,
As ragged as thy locks,

In dark Cimmerian desert ever
dwell.
But come, thou Goddess fair and free,
In Heaven yclept Euphrosyne,
And by men heart-easing Mirth ;
Whom lovely Venus, at a birth,
With two sister Graces more,
To ivy-crownèd Bacchus bore :
Or whether (as some sager sing)
The frolic wind that breathes the
spring,
Zephyr, with Aurora playing,
As he met her once a-Maying,
There, on beds of violets blue,
And fresh-blown roses washed in dew,
Filled her with thee, a daughter fair,
So buxom, blithe, and debonair.
Haste thee, Nymph, and bring with
thee

Jest, and youthful Jollity,
Quips and cranks and wanton wiles,
Nods and becks and wreathèd smiles,
Such as hang on Hebe's cheek,
And love to live in dimple sleek;
Sport that wrinkled Care derides,
And Laughter holding both his sides.
Come, and trip it, as you go,
On the light fantastic toe;
And in thy right hand lead with thee
The mountain-nymph, sweet Liberty;
And, if I give thee honour due,
Mirth, admit me of thy crew,
To live with her, and live with thee,
In unreproved pleasures free;
To hear the lark begin his flight,
And, singing, startle the dull night,
From his watch-tower in the skies,
Till the dappled dawn doth rise;

Then to come, in spite of sorrow,
And at my window bid good-morrow,
Through the sweer-briar or the vine,
Or the twisted eglantine ;
While the cock, with lively din,
Scatters the rear of darkness thin ;
And to the stack, or the barn-door,
Stoutly struts his dames before :
Oft listening how the hounds and horn
Cheerly rouse the slumbering morn,
From the side of some hoar hill,
Through the high wood echoing shrill :
Sometime walking, not unseen,
By hedgerow elms, on hillocks green,
Right against the eastern gate
Where the great Sun begins his state,
Robed in flames and amber light,
The clouds in thousand liveries dight ;

While the ploughman, near at hand,
Whistles o'er the furrowed land,
And the milkmaid singeth blithe,
And the mower whets his scythe,
And every shepherd tells his tale
Under the hawthorn in the dale.
Straight mine eye hath caught new
pleasures,
Whilst the landskip round it measures:
Russet lawns, and fallows grey,
Where the nibbling flocks do stray;
Mountains on whose barren breast
The labouring clouds do often rest;
Meadows trim, with daisies pied;
Shallow brooks, and rivers wide;
Towers and battlements it sees
Bosomed high in tufted trees,
Where perhaps some beauty lies,
The cynosure of neighbouring eyes.

Hard by a cottage chimney smokes
From betwixt two aged oaks,
Where Corydon and Thyrsis met,
Are at their savoury dinner set
Of herbs and other country messes,
Which the neat-handed Phyllis dresses;
And then in haste her bower she leaves,
With Thestylis to bind the sheaves;
Or, if the earlier season lead,
To the tanned haycock in the mead.
Sometimes, with secure delight,
The upland hamlets will invite,
When the merry bells ring round,
And the jocund rebecks sound
To many a youth and many a maid
Dancing in the chequered shade,
And young and old come forth to play
On a sunshine holiday,

Till the livelong daylight fail :
Then to the spicy nut-brown ale,
With stories told of many a feat,
How fairy Mab the junkets eat.
She was pinched and pulled, she said ;
And he, by Friar's lantern led,
Tells how the drudging goblin sweat
To earn his cream-bowl duly set,
When in one night, ere glimpse of
morn,
His shadowy flail hath threshed the
corn
That ten day-labourers could not end ;
Then lies him down, the lubber fiend,
And, stretched out all the chimney's
length,
Basks at the fire his hairy strength,
And crop-full out of doors he flings,
Ere the first cock his matin rings.

Thus done the tales, to bed they creep,
By whispering winds soon lulled asleep.
Towered cities please us then,
And the busy hum of men,
Where throngs of knights and barons bold,
In weeds of peace, high triumphs hold,
With store of ladies, whose bright eyes
Rain influence, and judge the prize
Of wit or arms, while both contend
To win her grace whom all commend.
There let Hymen oft appear
In saffron robe, with taper clear,
And pomp, and feast, and revelry,
With mask and antique pageantry;
Such sights as youthful poets dream
On summer eves by haunted stream.

Then to the well-trod stage anon,
If Jonson's learned sock be on,
Or sweetest Shakespeare, Fancy's child,
Warble his native wood-notes wild.
And ever, against eating cares,
Lap me in soft Lydian airs,
Married to immortal verse,
Such as the meeting soul may pierce,
In notes with many a winding bout
Of linkèd sweetness long drawn out
With wanton heed and giddy cunning,
The melting voice through mazes running,
Untwisting all the chains that tie
The hidden soul of harmony ;
That Orpheus' self may heave his head,
From golden slumber on a bed

Of heaped Elysian flowers, and hear
Such strains as would have won the
ear
Of Pluto to have quite set free
His half-regained Eurydice.
These delights if thou canst give,
Mirth, with thee I mean to live.

IL PENSEROSO

IL PENSEROSO.

HENCE, vain deluding Joys,
The brood of Folly without father bred!
How little you bested,
Or fill the fixèd mind with all your toys!
Dwell in some idle brain,
And fancies fond with gaudy shapes possess,
As thick and numberless
As the gay motes that people the sunbeams,
Or likest hovering dreams,

The fickle pensioners of Morpheus' train.
But, hail! thou Goddess sage and holy,
Hail, divinest Melancholy!
Whose saintly visage is too bright
To hit the sense of human sight,
And therefore to our weaker view,
O'erlaid with black, staid Wisdom's hue;
Black, but such as in esteem
Prince Memnon's sister might beseem,
Or that starred Ethiop queen that strove
To set her beauty's praise above
The Sea-Nymphs, and their powers offended.
Yet thou art higher far descended:
Thee bright-haired Vesta long of yore

To solitary Saturn bore ;
His daughter she ; in Saturn's reign
Such mixture was not held a stain.
Oft in glimmering bowers and glades
He met her, and in secret shades
Of woody Ida's inmost grove,
Whilst yet there was no fear of Jove.
Come, pensive Nun, devout and pure,
Sober, steadfast, and demure,
All in a robe of darkest grain,
Flowing with majestic train,
And sable stole of cypress lawn
Over thy decent shoulders drawn.
Come ; but keep thy wonted state,
With even step, and musing gait,
And looks commercing with the skies,
Thy rapt soul sitting in thine eyes :
There, held in holy passion still,
Forget thyself to marble, till

With a sad leaden downward cast
Thou fix them on the earth as fast.
And join with thee calm Peace and
Quiet,
Spare Fast, that oft with gods doth
diet,
And hears the Muses in a ring
Aye round about Jove's altar sing ;
And add to these retired Leisure,
That in trim gardens takes his pleas-
ure ;
But, first and chiefest, with thee bring
Him that yon soars on golden wing,
Guiding the fiery-wheelèd throne,
The Cherub Contemplation ;
And the mute Silence hist along,
'Less Philomel will deign a song,
In her sweetest saddest plight,
Smoothing the rugged brow of Night,

While Cynthia checks her dragon yoke
Gently o'er the accustomed oak.
Sweet bird, that shunn'st the noise of folly,
Most musical, most melancholy !
Thee, chauntress, oft the woods among,
I woo, to hear thy even-song ;
And, missing thee, I walk unseen
On the dry smooth-shaven green,
To behold the wandering moon,
Riding near her highest noon,
Like one that had been led astray
Through the heaven's wide pathless way,
And oft, as if her head she bowed,
Stooping through a fleecy cloud.
Oft, on a plat of rising ground,
I hear the far-off curfew sound,

Over some wide-watered shore,
Swinging slow with sullen roar ;
Or, if the air will not permit,
Some still removèd place will fit,
Where glowing embers through the
room
Teach light to counterfeit a gloom,
Far from all resort of mirth,
Save the cricket on the hearth,
Or the bellman's drowsy charm
To bless the doors from nightly harm.
Or let my lamp, at midnight hour,
Be seen in some high lonely tower,
Where I may oft outwatch the Bear,
With thrice great Hermes, or un-
sphere
The spirit of Plato, to unfold
What worlds or what vast regions
hold

The immortal mind that hath forsook
Her mansion in this fleshly nook ;
And of those demons that are found
In fire, air, flood, or underground,
Whose power hath a true consent,
With planet or with element.
Sometime let gorgeous Tragedy
In sceptred pall come sweeping by,
Presenting Thebes, or Pelops' line,
Or the tale of Troy divine,
Or what (though rare) of later age
Ennobled hath the buskined stage.
But, O sad Virgin ! that thy power
Might raise Musæus from his bower ;
Or bid the soul of Orpheus sing
Such notes as, warbled to the string,
Drew iron tears down Pluto's cheek,
And made Hell grant what love did
seek ;

Or call up him that left half-told
The story of Cambuscan bold,
Of Camball, and of Algarsife,
And who had Canace to wife,
That owned the virtuous ring and glass,
And of the wondrous horse of brass
On which the Tartar king did ride ;
And if aught else great bards beside
In sage and solemn tunes have sung,
Of turneys, and of trophies hung,
Of forests, and enchantments drear,
Where more is meant than meets the ear.
Thus, Night, oft see me in thy pale career,
Till civil-suited Morn appear,
Not tricked and frounced, as she was wont
With the Attic boy to hunt,

But kerchieft in a comely cloud,
While rocking winds are piping loud,
Or ushered with a shower still,
When the gust hath blown his fill,
Ending on the rustling leaves,
With minute-drops from off the eaves.
And, when the sun begins to fling
His flaring beams, me, Goddess, bring
To archèd walks of twilight groves,
And shadows brown, that Sylvan loves,
Of pine, or monumental oak,
Where the rude axe with heavèd stroke
Was never heard the nymphs to daunt,
Or fright them from their hallowed haunt.
There, in close covert, by some brook,
Where no profaner eye may look,
Hide me from day's garish eye,
While the bee with honeyed thigh,

That at her flowery work doth sing,
And the waters murmuring,
With such consort as they keep,
Entice the dewy-feathered Sleep.
And let some strange mysterious dream
Wave at his wings, in airy stream
Of lively portraiture displayed
Softly on my eyelids laid ;
And, as I wake, sweet music breathe
Above, about, or underneath,
Sent by some Spirit to mortals good,
Or the unseen Genius of the wood.
But let my due feet never fail
To walk the studious cloister's pale,
And love the high embowèd roof,
With antique pillars massy-proof,
And storied windows richly dight,
Casting a dim religious light.
There let the pealing organ blow,

To the full-voiced quire below,
In service high and anthems clear,
As may with sweetness, through mine
ear,
Dissolve me into ecstasies,
And bring all Heaven before mine eyes.
And may at last my weary age
Find out the peaceful hermitage,
The hairy gown and mossy cell,
Where I may sit and rightly spell
Of every star that heaven doth shew,
And every herb that sips the dew,
Till old experience do attain
To something like prophetic strain.
These pleasures, Melancholy, give;
And I with thee will choose to live.

SONNETS

SONNETS.

I.

TO THE NIGHTINGALE.

O NIGHTINGALE that on yon bloomy spray
Warblest at eve, when all the woods are still,
Thou with fresh hope the lover's heart dost fill,
While the jolly hours lead on propitious May.
Thy liquid notes that close the eye of day,

First heard before the shallow cuckoo's bill,
Portend success in love. O, if Jove's will
Have linked that amorous power to thy soft lay,
Now timely sing, ere the rude bird of hate
Foretell my hopeless doom, in some grove nigh ;
As thou from year to year hast sung too late
For my relief, yet hadst no reason why.
Whether the Muse or Love call thee his mate,
Both them I serve, and of their train am I.

II.

DONNA leggiadra, il cui bel nome onora
L'erbosa val di Reno e il nobil varco,
Bene è colui d' ogni valore scarco
Qual tuo spirto gentil non innamora,
Che dolcemente mostrasi di fuora
De' sui atti soavi giammai parco,
E i don', che son d' amor saette ed arco,
Là onde l' alta tua virtù s'infiora.
Quando tu vaga parli, o lieta canti,
Che mover possa duro alpestre legno,
Guardi ciascun agli occhi ed agli orecchi

L'entrata chi di te si truova indegno ;
Grazia sola di sù gli vaglia, innanti
Che 'l disio amoroso al cuor s' invecchi.

III.

QUAL in colle aspro, all' imbrunir di sera,
L' avezza giovinetta pastorella
Va bagnando l' erbetta strana e bella
Che mal si spande a disusata spera
Fuor di sua natia alma primavera,
Così Amor meco insù la lingua snella
Desta il fior novo di strania favella,
Mentre io di te, vezzosamente altera,
Canto, dal mio buon popol non inteso,
E 'l bel Tamigi cangio col bell' Arno.
Amor lo volse, ed io all' altrui peso

Seppi ch' Amor cosa mai volse indarno.
Deh ! foss' il mio cuor lento e 'l duro seno
A chi pianta dal ciel si buon terreno.

Canzone.

Ridonsi donne e giovani amorosi
M' accostandosi attorno, e "Perchè scrivi,
Perchè tu scrivi in lingua ignota e strana
Verseggiando d' amor, e come t' osi?
Dinne, se la tua speme sia mai vana,
E de' pensieri lo miglior t' arrivi!"
Così mi van burlando: "altri rivi,
Altri lidi t' aspettan, ed altre onde,
Nelle cui verdi sponde
Spuntati ad or ad or alla tua chioma
L' immortal guiderdon d' eterne frondi.

Perchè alle spalle tue soverchia
soma?"
Canzon, dirotti, e tu per me rispondi:
"Dice mia Donna, e 'l suo dir è il mio
cuore,
'Questa è lingua di cui si vanta
Amore.'"

IV.

DIODATI, (e te 'l dirò con maraviglia),
Quel ritroso io, ch' amor spreggiar solea
E de' suoi lacci spesso mi ridea,
Già caddi, ov' uom, dabben talor s' impigila
Nè treccie d' oro, nè guancia vermiglia
M' abbaglian sì, ma sotto nova idea
Pellegrina bellezza che 'l cuor bea,
Portamenti alti onesti, e nelle ciglia
Quel sereno fulgor d' amabil nero,
Parole adorne di lingua più d'una,
E 'l cantar che di mezzo l' emispero

Traviar ben può la faticosa Luna ;
  E degli occhi suoi avventa sì gran
    fuoco
  Che l' incerar gli orecchi mi fia poco.

V.

PER certo i bei vostr' occhi, Donna mia,
Esser non può che non sian lo mio sole;
Sì mi percuoton forte, come ei suole
Per l' arene di Libia chi s' invia,
Mentre un caldo vapor (nè sentì pria)
Da quel lato si spinge ove mi duole,
Che forse amanti nelle lor parole
Chiaman sospir; io non so che si sia.
Parte rinchiusa e turbida si cela
Scossomi il petto, e poi n' uscendo poco

Quivi d' attorno o s' agghiaccia o
s' ingiela ;
Ma quanto agli occhi giunge a trovar
loco
Tutte le notti a me suol far piovose,
Finchè mia alba rivien colma di
rose.

VI.

GIOVANE, piano, e semplicetto
amante,
Poichè fuggir me stesso in dubbio
sono,
Madonna, a voi del mio cuor l' umil
dono
Farò divoto. Io certo a prove tante
L' ebbi fedele, intrepido, costante,
Di pensieri leggiadro, accorto, e bu-
ono.
Quando rugge il gran mondo, e
scocca il tuono,
S' arma di se, e d' intero diamante,
Tanto del forse e d' invidia sicuro,

Di timori, e speranze al popol use,
Quanto d' ingegno e d' alto valor vago,
E di cetra sonora, e delle Muse :
Sol troverete in tal parte men duro
Ove Amor mise l' insanabil ago.

VII.

ON HIS HAVING ARRIVED AT THE AGE OF TWENTY-THREE.

HOW soon hath Time, the subtle thief of youth,
Stolen on his wing my three-and-twentieth year!
My hasting days fly on with full career,
But my late spring no bud or blossom shew'th.
Perhaps my semblance might deceive the truth,
That I to manhood am arrived so near;

And inward ripeness doth much less
appear,
That some more timely-happy spirits
endu'th.
Yet, be it less or more, or soon or
slow,
It shall be still in strictest measure
even
To that same lot, however mean or
high,
Toward which Time leads me, and
the will of Heaven
All is, if I have grace to use it so,
As ever in my great Task-Master's
eye.

VIII.

WHEN THE ASSAULT WAS INTENDED TO THE CITY.

CAPTAIN or Colonel, or Knight
in Arms,
Whose chance on these defenceless
doors may seize,
If deed of honour did thee ever
please,
Guard them, and him within protect
from harms.
He can requite thee; for he knows the
charms
That call fame on such gentle acts
as these,

And he can spread thy name o'er lands and seas,
Whatever clime the sun's bright circle warms.
Lift not thy spear against the Muses' bower:
The great Emathian conqueror bid spare
The house of Pindarus, when temple and tower
Went to the ground; and the repeated air
Of sad Electra's poet had the power
To save the Athenian walls from ruin bare.

IX.

TO THE LADY MARGARET LEY.

DAUGHTER to that good Earl, once President
Of England's Council and her Treasury,
Who lived in both unstained with gold or fee,
And left them both, more in himself content,
Till the sad breaking of that Parliament
Broke him, as that dishonest victory
At Chæronea, fatal to liberty,

Killed with report that old man eloquent,
Though later born than to have known the days
Wherein your father flourished, yet by you,
Madam, methinks I see him living yet :
So well your words his noble virtues praise
That all both judge you to relate them true
And to possess them, honoured Margaret.

X.

ON THE DETRACTION WHICH FOLLOWE] UPON MY WRITING CERTAIN TREATISES.

A BOOK was writ of late callec
Tetrachordon,
And woven close, both matter, form
and style ;
The subject new : it walked th(
town a while,
Numbering good intellects ; nov
seldom pored on.
Cries the stall-reader, " Bless us
what a word on
A title-page is this ! " ; and som(
in file

Stand spelling false, while one might
walk to Mile-
End Green. Why, is it harder, sirs,
than *Gordon*,
Colkitto, or *Macdonnel*, or *Galasp*?
Those rugged names to our like
mouths grow sleek
That would have made Quintilian
stare and gasp.
Thy age, like ours, O soul of Sir John
Cheek,
Hated not learning worse than toad
or asp,
When thou taught'st Cambridge and
King Edward Greek.

XI.

ON THE SAME.

I DID but prompt the age to quit their clogs
By the known rules of ancient liberty,
When straight a barbarous noise environs me
Of owls and cuckoos, asses, apes, and dogs;
As when those hinds that were transformed to frogs,
Railed at Latona's twin-born progeny,

Which after held the Sun and Moon
in fee.
But this is got by casting pearl to
hogs,
That bawl for freedom in their sense-
less mood,
And still revolt when Truth would
set them free.
Licence they mean when they cry
Liberty ;
For who loves that must first be wise
and good :
But from that mark how far they
rove we see,
For all this waste of wealth and loss
of blood.

XII.

TO A VIRTUOUS YOUNG LADY.

LADY, that in the prime of earliest youth
Wisely hast shunned the broad way and the green,
And with those few art eminently seen
That labour up the hill of heavenly Truth,
The better part with Mary and with Ruth
Chosen thou hast; and they that overween,

And at thy growing virtues fret their
spleen,
No anger find in thee, but pity and
ruth.
Thy care is fixed, and zealously attends
To fill thy odorous lamp with deeds
of light,
And hope that reaps not shame.
Therefore be sure
Thou, when the Bridegroom with his
feastful friends
Passes to bliss at the mid-hour of
night,
Hast gained thy entrance, Virgin
wise and pure.

XIII.

TO MR. H. LAWES, ON HIS AIRS.

HARRY, whose tuneful and well-measured song
First taught our English music how to span
Words with just note and accent, not to scan
With Midas' ears, committing short and long,
Thy worth and skill exempts thee from the throng,
With praise enough for Envy to look wan;

To after age thou shalt be writ the man
That with smooth air couldst humour best our tongue.
Thou honour'st Verse, and Verse must lend her wing
To honour thee, the priest of Phœbus' quire,
That tunest their happiest lines in hymn or story.
Dante shall give Fame leave to set thee higher
Than his Casella, whom he wooed to sing,
Met in the milder shades of Purgatory.

XIV.

ON THE RELIGIOUS MEMORY OF MRS. CATHERINE THOMSON, MY CHRISTIAN FRIEND, DECEASED DEC. 16, 1646.

WHEN Faith and Love, which parted from thee never,
Had ripened thy just soul to dwell with God,
Meekly thou didst resign this earthly load
Of death, called life, which us from life doth sever.
Thy works, and alms, and all thy good endeavour,

Stayed not behind, nor in the grave
were trod;
But, as Faith pointed with her
golden rod,
Followed thee up to joy and bliss
for ever.
Love led them on; and Faith, who
knew them best
Thy handmaids, clad them o'er with
purple beams
And azure wings, that up they flew
so drest,
And spake the truth of thee on glorious
themes
Before the Judge; who thenceforth
bid thee rest,
And drink thy fill of pure immortal
streams.

XV.

ON THE LORD GENERAL FAIRFAX, AT THE SIEGE OF COLCHESTER.

FAIRFAX, whose name in arms through Europe rings,
Filling each mouth with envy or with praise,
And all her jealous monarchs with amaze,
And rumours loud that daunt remotest kings,
Thy firm unshaken virtue ever brings
Victory home, though new rebellions raise

Their Hydra heads, and the false North displays
Her broken league to imp their serpent wings.
O yet a nobler task awaits thy hand
(For what can war but endless war still breed?)
Till truth and right from violence be freed,
And public faith cleared from the shameful brand
Of public fraud. In vain doth Valour bleed,
While Avarice and Rapine share the land.

XVI.

TO THE LORD GENERAL CROMWELL, MAY, 1652,

ON THE PROPOSALS OF CERTAIN MINISTERS AT THE COMMITTEE FOR PROPAGATION OF THE GOSPEL.

CROMWELL, our chief of men, who through a cloud
Not of war only, but detractions rude,
Guided by faith and matchless fortitude,
To peace and truth thy glorious way hast ploughed,
And on the neck of crowned Fortune proud

Hast reared God's trophies, and his work pursued,
While Darwen stream, with blood of Scots imbrued,
And Dunbar field, resounds thy praises loud,
And Worcester's laureate wreath : yet much remains
To conquer still ; Peace hath her victories
No less renowned than War : new foes arise,
Threatening to bind our souls with secular chains.
Help us to save free conscience from the paw
Of hireling wolves, whose Gospel is their maw.

XVII.

TO SIR HENRY VANE THE YOUNGER.

VANE, young in years, but in sage
counsel old,
Than whom a better senator ne'er
held
The helm of Rome, when gowns,
not arms, repelled
The fierce Epirot, and the African
bold,
Whether to settle peace, or to unfold
The drift of hollow states hard to be
spelled ;

Then to advise how war may best upheld
Move by her two main nerves, iron and gold,
In all her equipage ; besides, to know
Both spiritual power and civil, what each means,
What severs each, thou hast learned, which few have done.
The bounds of either sword to thee we owe :
Therefore on thy firm hand Religion leans
In peace, and reckons thee her eldest son.

XVIII.

ON THE LATE MASSACRE IN PIEDMONT.

AVENGE, O Lord, thy slaughtered saints, whose bones
Lie scattered on the Alpine mountains cold;
Even them who kept thy truth so pure of old,
When all our fathers worshiped stocks and stones,
Forget not: in thy book record their groans
Who were thy sheep, and in their ancient fold

Slain by the bloody Piedmontese, that rolled
Mother with infant down the rocks. Their moans
The vales redoubled to the hills, and they
To heaven. Their martyred blood and ashes sow
O'er all the Italian fields, where still doth sway
The triple Tyrant; that from these may grow
A hundredfold, who, having learnt thy way,
Early may fly the Babylonian woe.

XIX.

ON HIS BLINDNESS.

WHEN I consider how my light is spent
Ere half my days in this dark world and wide,
And that one talent which is death to hide
Lodged with me useless, though my soul more bent
To serve therewith my Maker, and present
My true account, lest He returning chide,

"Doth God exact day-labour, light denied?"
I fondly ask. But Patience, to prevent
That murmur, soon replies, "God doth not need
Either man's work or his own gifts. Who best
Bear his mild yoke, they serve him best. His state
Is kingly: thousands at his bidding speed,
And post o'er land and ocean without rest;
They also serve who only stand and wait."

XX.

TO MR. LAWRENCE.

LAWRENCE, of virtuous father virtuous son,
Now that the fields are dank, and ways are mire,
Where shall we sometimes meet, and by the fire
Help waste a sullen day, what may be won
From the hard season gaining? Time will run
On smoother, till Favonius reinspire

The frozen earth, and clothe in fresh attire
The lily and rose, that neither sowed nor spun.
What neat repast shall feast us, light and choice,
Of Attic taste, with wine, whence we may rise
To hear the lute well touched, or artful voice
Warble immortal notes and Tuscan air?
He who of those delights can judge, and spare
To interpose them oft, is not unwise.

XXI.

TO CYRIACK SKINNER.

CYRIACK, whose grandsire on the royal bench
Of British Themis, with no mean applause,
Pronounced, and in his volumes taught, our laws,
Which others at their bar so often wrench,
To-day deep thoughts resolve with me to drench
In mirth that after no repenting draws;

Let Euclid rest, and Archimedes pause,
And what the Swede intend, and what the French.
To measure life learn thou betimes, and know
Toward solid good what leads the nearest way ;
For other things mild Heaven a time ordains,
And disapproves that care, though wise in show,
That with superfluous burden loads the day,
And, when God sends a cheerful hour, refrains.

XXII.

TO THE SAME.

CYRIACK, this three years' day
these eyes, though clear,
To outward view, of blemish or of
spot,
Bereft of light, their seeing have
forgot;
Nor to their idle orbs doth sight
appear
Of sun, or moon, or star, throughout
the year,
Or man, or woman. Yet I argue
not

Against Heaven's hand or will, nor bate a jot
Of heart or hope; but still bear up and steer
Right onward. What supports me, dost thou ask?
The conscience, friend, to have lost them overplied
In Liberty's defence, my noble task,
Of which all Europe rings from side to side.
This thought might lead me through the world's vain mask
Content, though blind, had I no better guide.

XXIII.

ON HIS DECEASED WIFE.

METHOUGHT I saw my late espoused saint
Brought to me like Alcestis from the grave,
Whom Jove's great son to her glad husband gave,
Rescued from Death by force, though pale and faint.
Mine, as whom washed from spot of child-bed taint
Purification in the Old Law did save,

And such as yet once more I trust to have
Full sight of her in Heaven without restraint,
Came vested all in white, pure as her mind.
Her face was veiled ; yet to my fancied sight
Love, sweetness, goodness, in her person shined
So clear as in no face with more delight.
But, oh ! as to embrace me she inclined,
I waked, she fled, and day brought back my night.

ODES

ODES.

I.

ON THE MORNING OF CHRIST'S NATIVITY.

Composed 1629.

I.

THIS is the month, and this the
 happy morn,
Wherein the Son of Heaven's Eternal
 King,
Of wedded maid and virgin mother
 born,
Our great redemption from above did
 bring;
For so the holy sages once did sing,

That he our deadly forfeit should
release,
And with his Father work us a per-
petual peace.

II.

That glorious form, that light unsuf-
ferable,
And that far-beaming blaze of maj-
esty;
Wherewith he wont at Heaven's high
council-table
To sit the midst of Trinal Unity,
He laid aside, and, here with us to be,
Forsook the courts of everlasting
day,
And chose with us a darksome house
of mortal clay.

III.

Say, Heavenly Muse, shall not thy
sacred vein
Afford a present to the Infant God?
Hast thou no verse, no hymn, or
solemn strain,
To welcome him to this his new abode,
Now while the heaven, by the Sun's
team untrod,
Hath took no print of the approach-
ing light,
And all the spangled host keep watch
in squadrons bright?

IV.

See how from far upon the eastern road
The star-led wizards haste with odours
sweet!

Oh ! run ; prevent them with thy
humble ode,
And lay it lowly at his blessed feet ;
Have thou the honour first thy Lord to
greet,
And join thy voice unto the Angel
Quire,
From out his secret altar touched with
hallowed fire.

The Hymn.

I.

It was the winter wild,
While the heaven-born child
All meanly wrapt in the rude
manger lies ;
Nature, in awe to him,
Had doffed her gaudy trim,

With her great Master so to sympathise:
It was no season then for her
To wanton with the Sun, her lusty paramour.

II.

Only with speeches fair
She woos the gentle air
To hide her guilty front with innocent snow;
And on her naked shame,
Pollute with sinful blame,
The saintly veil of maiden white to throw;
Confounded, that her Maker's eyes
Should look so near upon her foul deformities.

III.

But he, her fears to cease,
Sent down the meek-eyed Peace:
She, crowned with olive green, came softly sliding
Down through the turning sphere,
His ready harbinger,
With turtle wing the amorous clouds dividing;
And, waving wide her myrtle wand,
She strikes a universal peace through sea and land.

IV.

No war, or battle's sound,
Was heard the world around;
The idle spear and shield were high uphung;
The hookèd chariot stood

Unstained with hostile blood;
The trumpet spake not to the armèd throng;
And kings sat still with awful eye,
As if they surely knew their sovran Lord was by.

V.

But peaceful was the night
Wherein the Prince of Light
His reign of peace upon the earth began.
The winds, with wonder whist,
Smoothly the waters kissed,
Whispering new joys to the mild Ocean,
Who now hath quite forgot to rave,
While birds of calm sit brooding on the charmèd wave.

VI.

The stars, with deep amaze,
Stand fixed in steadfast gaze,
Bending one way their precious influence;
And will not take their flight,
For all the morning light,
Or Lucifer that often warned them thence;
But in their glimmering orbs did glow,
Until their Lord himself bespake, and bid them go.

VII.

And, though the shady gloom
Had given day her room,
The Sun himself withheld his wonted speed,

And hid his head for shame,
As his inferior flame
The new-enlightened world no more should need:
He saw a greater Sun appear
Than his bright throne or burning axletree could bear.

VIII.

The shepherds on the lawn,
Or ere the point of dawn,
Sat simply chatting in a rustic row;
Full little thought they then
That the mighty Pan
Was kindly come to live with them below:
Perhaps their loves, or else their sheep,
Was all that did their silly thoughts so busy keep.

IX.

When such music sweet
Their hearts and ears did greet
As never was by mortal finger strook,
Divinely-warbled voice
Answering the stringed noise,
As all their souls in blissful rapture took :
The air, such pleasure loth to lose,
With thousand echoes still prolongs each heavenly close.

X.

Nature, that heard such sound
Beneath the hollow round
Of Cynthia's seat the airy region thrilling,
Now was almost won

To think her part was done,
And that her reign had here its last fulfilling:
She knew such hàrmony alone
Could hold all Heaven and Earth in happier union.

XI.

At last surrounds their sight
A globe of circular light,
That with long beams the shame-faced Night arrayed;
The helmèd cherubim
And sworded seraphim,
Are seen in glittering ranks with wings displayed,
Harping in loud and solemn quire,
With unexpressive notes to Heaven's new-born Heir.

XII.

Such music (as 'tis said)
Before was never made,
But when of old the Sons of Morning sung,
While the Creator great
His constellations set,
And the well-balanced World on hinges hung,
And cast the dark foundations deep,
And bid the weltering waves their oozy channel keep.

XIII.

Ring out, ye crystal spheres !
Once bless our human ears,
If ye have power to touch our senses so ;
And let your silver chime

Move in melodious time;
And let the bass of heaven's deep
organ blow;
And with your ninefold harmony
Make up full consort to the angelic
symphony.

XIV.

For, if such holy song
Enwrap our fancy long,
Time will run back and fetch the
Age of Gold;
And speckled Vanity
Will sicken soon and die,
And leprous Sin will melt from
earthly mould;
And Hell itself will pass away,
And leave her dolorous mansions to
the peering day.

XV.

Yea, Truth and Justice then
Will down return to men,
Orbed in a rainbow; and, like glories wearing,
Mercy will sit between,
Throned in celestial sheen,
With radiant feet the tissued clouds down steering;
And Heaven, as at some festival,
Will open wide the gates of her high palace-hall.

XVI.

But wisest Fate says No,
This must not yet be so;
The Babe yet lies in smiling infancy
That on the bitter cross

Must redeem our loss,
So both himself and us to glorify :
Yet first, to those ychained in sleep,
The wakeful trump of doom must
thunder through the deep,

XVII.

With such a horrid clang
As on Mount Sinai rang,
While the red fire and smouldering
clouds outbrake :
The aged Earth, aghast,
With terror of that blast,
Shall from the surface to the centre
shake,
When, at the world's last session,
The dreadful Judge in middle air shall
spread his throne.

XVIII.

And then at last our bliss
Full and perfect is,
But now begins; for, from this happy day,
The Old Dragon under ground
In straiter limits bound,
Not half so far casts his usurpèd sway,
And, wroth to see his kingdom fail,
Swinges the scaly horror of his folded tail.

XIX.

The Oracles are dumb;
No voice or hideous hum
Runs through the archèd roof in words deceiving.
Apollo from his shrine

Can no more divine,
With hollow shriek the steep of Delphos leaving.
No nightly trance, or breathèd spell,
Inspires the pale-eyed priest from the prophetic cell.

XX.

The lonely mountains o'er,
And the resounding shore,
A voice of weeping heard and loud lament;
From haunted spring, and dale
Edged with poplar pale,
The parting Genius is with sighing sent;
With flower-inwoven tresses torn
The Nymphs in twilight shade of tangled thickets mourn.

XXI.

In consecrated earth,
And on the holy hearth,
The Lars and Lemures moan with midnight plaint;
In urns, and altars round,
A drear and dying sound
Affrights the flamens at their service quaint;
And the chill marble seems to sweat,
While each peculiar Power forgets his wonted seat.

XXII.

Peor and Baälim
Forsake their temples dim,
With that twice-battered God of Palestine;
And moonèd Ashtaroth,

Heaven's queen and mother both,
  Now sits not girt with tapers' holy
    shine:
The Libyc Hammon shrinks his horn;
In vain the Tyrian maids their wound-
    ed Thammuz mourn.

XXIII.

And sullen Moloch, fled,
Hath left in shadows dread
  His burning idol all of blackest
    hue;
In vain with cymbal's ring
They call the grisly king,
  In dismal dance about the furnace
    blue;
The brutish gods of Nile as fast,
Isis, and Orus, and the dog Anubis,
    haste.

XXIV.

Nor is Osiris seen
In Memphian grove or green,
Trampling the unshowered grass with lowings loud;
Nor can he be at rest
Within his sacred chest;
Nought but profoundest Hell can be his shroud;
In vain, with timbreled anthems dark,
The sable-stolèd sorcerers bear his worshiped ark.

XXV.

He feels from Juda's land
The dreaded Infant's hand;
The rays of Bethlehem blind his dusky eyn;
Nor all the gods beside

Longer dare abide,
Nor Typhon huge ending in snaky
twine :
Our Babe, to show his Godhead true,
Can in his swaddling bands control
the damnèd crew.

XXVI.

So, when the sun in bed
Curtained with cloudy red,
Pillows his chin upon an orient
wave,
The flocking shadows pale
Troop to the infernal jail,
Each fettered ghost slips to his
several grave,
And the yellow-skirted fays
Fly after the night-steeds, leaving
their moon-loved maze.

XXVII.

But see! the Virgin blest
Hath laid her Babe to rest.
Time is our tedious song should
here have ending:
Heaven's youngest-teemèd star
Hath fixed her polished car,
Her sleeping Lord with handmaid
lamp attending;
And all about the courtly stable
Bright-harnessed Angels sit in order
serviceable.

II.

ON THE PASSION.

I.

EREWHILE of music, and ethereal
 mirth,
Wherewith the stage of air and earth
 did ring,
And joyous news of Heavenly Infant's
 birth,
My muse with Angels did divide to
 sing;
But headlong joy is ever on the
 wing,

In wintry solstice like the shortened light
Soon swallowed up in dark and long outliving night.

II.

For now to sorrow must I tune my song,
And set my harp to notes of saddest woe,
Which on our dearest Lord did seize ere long,
Dangers, and snares, and wrongs, and worse than so,
Which he for us did freely undergo:
Most perfect Hero, tried in heaviest plight
Of labours huge and hard, too hard for human wight!

III.

He, sovran Priest, stooping his regal
head
That dropt with odorous oil down his
fair eyes,
Poor fleshly tabernacle enterèd,
His starry front low-roofed beneath the
skies :
Oh, what a mask was there, what a
disguise !
Yet more : the stroke of death he
must abide ;
Then lies him meekly down fast by
his brethren's side.

IV.

These latest scenes confine my roving
verse,
To this horizon is my Phœbus bound.

His godlike acts, and his temptations fierce,
And former sufferings, otherwhere are found;
Loud o'er the rest Cremona's trump doth sound:
Me softer airs befit, and softer strings
Of lute, or viol still, more apt for mournful things.

V.

Befriend me, Night, best patroness of grief!
Over the pole thy thickest mantle throw,
And work my flattered fancy to belief,
That heaven and earth are coloured with my woe;

My sorrows are too dark for day to
know:
The leaves should all be black
whereon I write,
And letters, where my tears have
washed, a wannish white.

VI.

See, see the chariot, and those rushing
wheels,
That whirled the prophet up at Chebar
flood;
My spirit some transporting cherub
feels
To bear me where the towers of Salem
stood,
Once glorious towers, now sunk in
guiltless blood.

There doth my soul in holy vision sit,
In pensive trance, and anguish, and ecstastic fit.

VII.

Mine eye hath found that sad sepulchral rock
That was the casket of Heaven's richest store,
And here, though grief my feeble hands up-lock,
Yet on the softened quarry would I score
My plaining verse as lively as before;
For sure so well instructed are my tears
That they would fitly fall in ordered characters.

VIII.

Or, should I thence, hurried on viewless wing,
Take up a weeping on the mountains wild,
The gentle neighbourhood of grove and spring
Would soon unbosom all their echoes mild;
And I (for grief is easily beguiled)
Might think the infection of my sorrows loud
Had got a race of mourners on some pregnant cloud.

This Subject the Author finding to be above the years he had when he wrote it, and nothing satisfied with what was begun, left it unfinished.

III.

ON THE CIRCUMCISION.

YE flaming Powers, and wingèd
Warriors bright,
That erst with music, and triumphant
song,
First heard by happy watchful shep-
herds' ear,
So sweetly sung your joy the clouds
along,
Through the soft silence of the listen-
ing night,
Now mourn; and, if sad share with us
to bear

Your fiery essence can distil no
tear,
Burn in your sighs, and borrow
Seas wept from our deep sorrow.
He who with all Heaven's heraldry
whilere
Entered the world now bleeds to give
us ease.
Alas! how soon our sin
Sore doth begin
His infancy to seize!

O more exceeding love, or law more
just?
Just law, indeed, but more exceeding
love!
For we, by rightful doom remediless,
Were lost in death, till he, that dwelt
above,

High-throned in secret bliss, for us
 frail dust
Emptied his glory, even to naked-
 ness;
And that great covenant which we
 still transgress
Entirely satisfied,
And the full wrath beside
Of vengeful justice bore for our excess.
And seals obedience first with wound-
 ing smart
This day; but oh! ere long,
 Huge pangs and strong
 Will pierce more near his heart.

IV.

ON THE DEATH OF A FAIR INFANT DYING OF A COUGH.

Anno ætatis 17.

I.

O FAIREST flower, no sooner blown but blasted,
Soft silken primrose fading timelessly,
Summer's chief honour, if thou hadst outlasted
Bleak Winter's force that made thy blossom dry;
For he, being amorous on that lovely dye

That did thy cheek envermeil,
thought to kiss,
But killed, alas! and then bewailed his
fatal bliss.

II.

For, since grim Aquilo, his charioteer,
By boisterous rape the Athenian damsel got,
He thought it touched his deity full
near,
If likewise he some fair one wedded
not,
Thereby to wipe away the infamous
blot
Of long uncoupled bed and childless
eld,
Which 'mongst the wanton gods a
foul reproach was held.

III.

So, mounting up in icy-pearlèd car,
Through middle empire of the freezing
air
He wandered long, till thee he spied
from far ;
There ended was his quest, there
ceased his care :
Down he descended from his snow-soft
chair,
But, all unwares, with his cold-kind
embrace,
Unhoused thy virgin soul from her fair
biding-place.

IV.

Yet thou art not inglorious in thy
fate ;
For so Apollo, with unweeting hand,

Whilom did slay his dearly-lovèd
mate,
Young Hyacinth, born on Eurotas'
strand,
Young Hyacinth, the pride of Spartan
land;
But then transform'd him to a purple flower:
Alack, that so to change thee Winter
had no power!

V.

Yet can I not persuade me thou art
dead,
Or that thy corse corrupts in earth's
dark womb,
Or that thy beauties lie in wormy bed,
Hid from the world in a low-delvèd
tomb;

Could Heaven, for pity, thee so strictly doom ?
Oh no ! for something in thy face did shine
Above mortality, that showed thou wast divine.

VI.

Resolve me, then, O Soul most surely blest
(If so it be that thou these plaints dost hear) !
Tell me, bright Spirit, where'er thou hoverest,
Whether above that high first-moving sphere,
Or in the Elysian fields (if such there were),

Oh, say me true if thou wert mortal wight,
And why from us so quickly thou didst take thy flight.

VII.

Wert thou some star, which from the ruined roof
Of shaked Olympus by mischance didst fall;
Which careful Jove in nature's true behoof
Took up, and in fit place did reinstall?
Or did of late Earth's sons besiege the wall
Of sheeny Heaven, and thou some goddess fled
Amongst us here below to hide thy nectared head?

VIII.

Or wert thou that just maid who once
before
Forsook the hated earth, oh! tell me
sooth,
And camest again to visit us once
more?
Or wert thou [Mercy], that sweet-
smiling Youth?
Or that crowned Matron, sage white-
robèd Truth?
Or any other of that heavenly brood
Let down in cloudy throne to do the
world some good?

IX.

Or wert thou of the golden-wingèd host,
Who, having clad thyself in human
weed,

To earth from thy prefixèd seat didst
post,
And after short abode fly back with
speed,
As if to show what creatures Heaven
doth breed ;
Thereby to set the hearts of men on
fire
To scorn the sordid world, and unto
Heaven aspire ?

X.

But, oh ! why didst thou not stay here
below
To bless us with thy heaven-loved
innocence,
To slake his wrath whom sin hath
made our foe,

To turn swift-rushing black perdition
hence,
Or drive away the slaughtering pesti-
lence,
To stand 'twixt us and our deserved
smart?
But thou canst best perform that office
where thou art.

XI.

Then thou, the mother of so sweet a
child,
Her false-imagined loss cease to lament,
And wisely learn to curb thy sorrows
wild;
Think what a present thou to God
hast sent,

And render him with patience what
he lent:
This if thou do, he will an offspring
give,
That till the world's last end shall
make thy name to live.

V.

ON TIME.

FLY, envious Time, till thou run out thy race:
Call on the lazy leaden-stepping Hours,
Whose speed is but the heavy plummet's pace;
And glut thyself with what thy womb devours,
Which is no more than what is false and vain,
And merely mortal dross;
So little is our loss,

So little is thy gain !
For, when as each thing bad thou hast entombed,
And, last of all, thy greedy self consumed,
Then long Eternity shall greet our bliss
With an individual kiss,
And Joy shall overtake us as a flood ;
When every thing that is sincerely good
And perfectly divine,
With Truth, and Peace, and Love, shall ever shine
About the supreme throne
Of Him, to whose happy-making sight alone
When once our heavenly-guided soul shall climb,

Then, all this earthly grossness quit,
Attired with stars we shall for ever sit,
Triumphing over Death, and Chance,
and thee, O Time !

VI.

AT A SOLEMN MUSIC.

BLEST pair of Sirens, pledges of
Heaven's joy,
Sphere-born harmonious sisters, Voice
and Verse,
Wed your divine sounds, and mixed
power employ,
Dead things with inbreathed sense able
to pierce;
And to our high-raised phantasy pre-
sent
That undisturbèd song of pure con-
sent,

Aye sung before the sapphire-coloured
throne
To Him that sits thereon,
With saintly shout and solemn jubi-
lee ;
Where the bright Seraphim in burn-
ing row
Their loud uplifted angel-trumpets
blow,
And the Cherubic host, in thousand
quires
Touch their immortal harps of golden
wires,
With these just Spirits that wear victo-
rious palms,
Hymns devout and holy psalms
Singing everlastingly :
That we on Earth, with undiscording
voice,

May rightly answer that melodious
noise;
As once we did, till disproportioned
sin
Jarred against nature's chime, and
with harsh din
Broke the fair music that all creatures
made
To their great Lord, whose love their
motion swayed
In perfect diapason, whilst they stood
In first obedience, and their state of
good.
O, may we soon again renew that song,
And keep in tune with Heaven, till
God ere long
To his celestial concert us unite,
To live with Him, and sing in endless
morn of light!

VII.

AN EPITAPH ON THE MARCHIONESS OF WINCHESTER.

THIS rich marble doth inter
The honoured wife of Winchester,
A Viscount's daughter, an Earl's heir,
Besides what her virtues fair
Added to her noble birth,
More than she could own from Earth.
Summers three times eight save one
She has told ; alas ! too soon,
After so short time of breath,
To house with darkness and with death !

Yet, had the number of her days
Been as complete as was her praise,
Nature and Fate had had no strife
In giving limit to her life.
Her high birth and her graces sweet
Quickly found a lover meet;
The virgin quire for her request
The god that sits at marriage-feast;
He at their invoking came,
But with a scarce well-lighted flame;
And in his garland, as he stood,
Ye might discern a cypress-bud.
Once had the early matrons run
To greet her of a lovely son,
And now with second hope she goes,
And calls Lucina to her throes;
But, whether by mischance or blame,
Atropos for Lucina came;
And with remorseless cruelty

Spoiled at once both fruit and tree.
The hapless babe before his birth
Had burial, yet not laid in earth ;
And the languished mother's womb
Was not long a living tomb.
So have I seen some tender slip,
Saved with care from winter's nip,
The pride of her carnation train,
Plucked up by some unheedy swain,
Who only thought to crop the flower
New shot up from vernal shower ;
But the fair blossom hangs the head
Sideways, as on a dying bed,
And those pearls of dew she wears
Prove to be presaging tears
Which the sad morn had let fall
On her hastening funeral.
Gentle Lady, may thy grave
Peace and quiet ever have !

After this thy travail sore,
Sweet rest seize thee evermore,
That, to give the world increase,
Shortened hast thy own life's lease!
Here, besides the sorrowing
That thy noble house doth bring,
Here be tears of perfect moan
Wept for thee in Helicon;
And some flowers and some bays
For thy hearse, to strew the ways,
Sent thee from the banks of Came,
Devoted to thy virtuous name;
Whilst thou, bright Saint, high sitt'st
in glory,
Next her, much like to thee in story,
That fair Syrian shepherdess
Who, after years of barrenness,
The highly-favoured Joseph bore
To him that served for her before,

And at her next birth, much like thee,
Through pangs fled to felicity,
Far within the bosom bright
Of blazing Majesty and Light:
There with thee, new-welcome Saint,
Like fortunes may her soul acquaint,
With thee there clad in radiant sheen,
No Marchioness, but now a Queen.

VIII.

SONG ON MAY MORNING.

NOW the bright morning-star, Day's
harbinger,
Comes dancing from the east, and
leads with her
The flowery May, who from her green
lap throws
The yellow cowslip and the pale
primrose.
Hail, bounteous May, that dost in-
spire
Mirth, and youth, and warm desire!
Woods and groves are of thy dress-
ing;

Hill and dale doth boast thy blessing.
Thus we salute thee with our early song,
And welcome thee, and wish thee long.

THE END.

THIRD SERIES:

Lyrics. By Robert Browning.

Legend of Sleepy Hollow. By Washington Irving.

Pre-Raphaelitism. By John Ruskin.

Rime of the Ancient Mariner, and Cristabel. By S. T. Coleridge.

Speeches on America. By John Bright.

Education of Children. By Montaigne.

FOURTH SERIES:

The Rivals. By Richard Brinsley Sheridan.

Rip Van Winkle, and Wolfert's Roost. By Washington Irving.

L'Allegro, and Il Penseroso, together with the Sonnets and Odes. By John Milton.

Charity and Humor, and Nil Nisi Bonum. By William Makepeace Thackeray.

Elegy Written in a Country Churchyard, together with a Selection from the Odes and Sonnets. By Thomas Gray.

Thanatopsis, The Flood of Years, Lines to a Waterfowl, and Little People of the Snow. By William Cullen Bryant.

G. P. PUTNAM'S SONS, Publishers
NEW YORK AND LONDON

Literary Gems

The following "Gems" are bound in vellum cloth, white and gold, gilt top, rough edges. Each volume has a frontispiece in photogravure.

Price per set of two volumes, in flat box, $1.00

No. 1 { **Gold Bug**—POE.
Good-Natured Man—GOLDSMITH.

No. 2 { **Sonnets from the Portuguese**—BROWNING.
Lyrics—ROBERT BROWNING.

No. 3 { **Our Best Society**—CURTIS.
Nothing to Wear—BUTLER.

No. 4 { **Nibelungen Lied**—CARLYLE.
Science of History—FROUDE.

No. 5 { **Rab and His Friends**—BROWN.
King of the Golden River—RUSKIN.

No. 6 { **Rip Van Winkle**—IRVING.
Legend of Sleepy Hollow—IRVING.

No. 7 { **School for Scandal**—SHERIDAN.
The Rivals—SHERIDAN.

No. 8 { **The Culprit Fay**—DRAKE.
L'Allegro—MILTON.

No. 9 { **Sweetness and Light**—ARNOLD.
Charity and Humor—THACKERAY.

No. 10 { **Elegy**—GRAY.
Thanatopsis—BRYANT.

The above volumes are also sold separately at 50 cents.

www.ingramcontent.com/pod-product-compliance
Lightning Source LLC
LaVergne TN
LVHW021409110826
845150LV00007B/1843

* 9 7 8 1 4 2 5 5 1 1 4 2 5 *